SPIRITUAL VIGILANTES

The Truth Behind
the Attempted Destruction of God's Law

DANNY SHELTON

DLS Publishing, Inc.

www.dannyshelton.com

Editor: Bobby Davis, Yvonne Lewis
Cover / Inside Design: Chrystique Neibauer

Additional copies of this book are available through www.dannyshelton.com.
You can also order through 3ABN by calling (618) 627-4651 or visiting www.3ABNstore.com.

All scripture is quoted from the KJV or NKJV.

Scriptures quoted from the KJV are taken from the
KING JAMES VERSION (KJV): KING JAMES VERSION, public domain.

Scriptures quoted from NKJV are from The New King James Version,
copyright © 1979, 1980, 1982 by Thomas Nelson, Inc., Publishers.

Library of Congress Cataloging-in-Publication Data:

ISBN 13: 978-1-942455-30-1

CONTENTS

CONTENTS

SPIRITUAL
VIGILANTES

INTRODUCTION

The book you are about to read is definitely a departure from any of the others I have written or co-written in the past. But as a Christian and an American, I feel compelled by God to write a "tell it like it is" book. It is a straightforward, "no holds barred" type of book. You will see that I have purposely thrown out political correctness at the risk of offending any number of readers, but I would rather offend people than our Creator God of the Universe.

America is on the road to national ruin! More than ever before, we live in a time where many of our government and church leaders have embraced the standards of political correctness in lieu of the law of God. My target readers are those who identify as Christians, believe in the Bible, and attempt to live their lives in accordance with it.

Political correctness has taken over American politics—and the Christian church! As Christians, we need to become spiritual warriors in the army of Christ. Now is the time to stand up and be counted on the side of truth, while we still have religious liberty.

This book is entitled *Spiritual Vigilantes*. As you already know, there are physical vigilantes who place themselves above the law. We've all heard of individuals or rogue groups of people, including on occasion, law enforcement officers, who take the law into their own hands. They become judge, jury, and executioners of their victims, dealing out punishment ranging from physical and mental harm to murder!

This book contains examples of individuals or groups I call "Spiritual Vigilantes," who place themselves above the spiritual law of God and attempt to change or negate the very principles of life given to man—the Ten Commandments, written by the finger of God.

CHAPTER
I

AMERICA'S DOWNWARD SPIRAL

I think most of you will agree that America is extremely divided right now—unlike anything I've witnessed in my lifetime. I'm a baby boomer. Most people from my generation believe life was a lot simpler, and people seemed to get along much better with their neighbors in the past, when we lived by the mantra of "Right is right, and wrong is wrong."

Children anticipated living in better economic conditions than their parents, America was the greatest superpower on Earth, and everyone had full expectations of seeing their dreams and ambitions come true. There was prayer in schools, and every school-aged child in America started the morning off with the Pledge of Allegiance to the flag.

Television was entertaining, and, for the most part, morally clean. It was the world of *Leave It to Beaver* and *I Love Lucy*. Kids in America were not exposed to nudity and bad language through television and radio; and, of course, social media was not even a dream.

On American radio and television, the Christian movement had Billy Graham and Oral Roberts, and soon many other evangelists joined them—giving birth to the term, *televangelist*. With the Bible as their guide, they taught that smoking cigarettes, drinking alcohol, and living together before marriage was a sin! The Christian church was alive and well.

But Then Something Changed
The counter-culture group that called themselves hippies brought about a tremendous change in the 1960s. Those who joined this cultish movement rebelled against what they called "the establishment"—our systems of government and education, the police, the church, and anyone or anything that stood in the way of their New Age agenda and mantra: "If it feels good, do it!"

Suddenly, America's youth were exposed to illegal drugs, sexual promiscuity, and disrespect for God and country on a national scale. Meanwhile, Black Americans began to ban together to address the inequalities of American society. Shamefully segregated from mainstream whites, Black Americans were forced into substandard living conditions and an inferior educational system. Martin Luther King, Jr.—a young Black preacher—stepped forward to attract attention to the needs of Black America and gave birth to the Civil Rights Movement.

Not only were the hippie and Civil Rights movements reshaping America's social culture, but they brought in a jarring change to our music culture as well. Gone was the popularity of the easy listening music of Benny Goodman, Glenn Miller, Duke Ellington, Tommy Dorsey, Bing Crosby, and Doris Day. The Beatles, B.B. King, and Elvis—the King of Rock and Roll—came blasting to the forefront.

Most Americans were caught off guard by the hippie counterculture ideology, the civil rights protests, and the organized "coming out" of homosexuals that followed. Adding to the confusion, widespread protests of the Vietnam War were taking place, and thousands of draft dodgers refused to serve their country when called on by the government.

Unrest was spreading across our nation's college campuses like wildfire, and the resulting political backlash threatened the very heart of America's democracy. From John F. Kennedy's assassination to Richard Nixon's Watergate scandal, many were expecting America to crumble to her knees!

By the 1970s, this country was experiencing tremendous birth pains as she was about to deliver more of what I call the "Generation Gap Babies"—millions of young Americans from all cultural backgrounds who could no longer identify with their parents, the government, or their church because of the impact of a rapidly changing society.

What's the Problem?
Over the last 40 to 50 years, America has made great strides toward racial equality and the entertainment industry reflects this change as minority TV and movie stars, singers, and musicians have gained popularity. Minority athletes, and even brain surgeons like Dr. Ben Carson, receive worldwide acclaim. Many minority politicians have held, and currently hold, publicly elected offices—from local, state, and federal government positions up to, and including, the President of the United States of America! Still, for all our progress in the fight for equality, race remains a hot button issue.

I want to plant a seed here for readers who are Christians: *America's biggest problem is not a skin problem, but a sin problem* ("He who has an ear, let him hear . . .")! The past four or five decades have revealed something startling: America has suffered a great spiritual decline. As an example, *Leave It to Beaver* and *I Love Lucy* have been replaced with TV programs like *Sex in the City* and *Modern Family* (featuring a gay couple as main characters). The liberal media has

11

reshaped the values of modern society by inundating viewers with homosexual relationships as representative of normal family life. Many have become so desensitized to biblical truth that same-sex marriage has been legislated, and is now deemed acceptable. However, the Bible is clear that marriage is a holy union between one man and one woman—instituted by God during Creation Week when He created Adam and Eve. The marriage of the first couple is found in the first chapter of the Bible: "So God created man in His own image; in the image of God He created him; male and female He created them. Then God blessed them, and God said to them, 'Be fruitful and multiply; fill the earth.'" Genesis 1:27–28. (For more about the institution of marriage, read Genesis 2:21–24.)

Over the last several years, taxpayer dollars have been used by the federal government's public school system to promote Lesbian, Gay, Bisexual, Transgender, and Questioning (LGBTQ) clubs that encourage young students, starting in grade school, to experiment with homosexual relationships![1] Their platform gained support from our lawmakers when it began to be marketed as a program to help stop bullying in schools.

More Division
In 1973, by denying many state and federal restrictions on abortion in the United States, Roe v. Wade reshaped national politics and divided America into pro-abortion and anti-abortion groups—a deep division that still exists today.

The sixth commandment, found in Exodus 20, says, "You shall not murder." This commandment, written by God, the Creator of life, could not be clearer! It's straight to the point: *Murder is a sin against our fellow man and against God.*

As you can see, Americans are divided by race, religion, and politics like never before. The devil is very cunning—his

---

[1] Wikipedia.org, "Kevin Jennings," https://en.wikipedia.org/wiki/Kevin_Jennings (accessed 5/15/17).

agenda is to divide and conquer! As a country, we have fallen into his trap. Rather than coming together in the common interests of truth, honesty, and integrity, people continue to fight for their own selfish agendas.

CHAPTER
II

TEN COMMANDMENTS
VS. POLITICAL CORRECTNESS

Contrary to popular belief, America is not, and never has been, a Christian nation. However, America's Founding Fathers adopted the last six of the Ten Commandments as the foundation for our government. No nation can exist for long in peace, harmony, and safety, without following them.

Under the United States Constitution, these six moral laws, detailing man's duty to man, became the supreme law of the land. But as we'll find in the next few chapters, under tremendous pressure from the liberal left, our government has compromised God's laws by order of the United States Supreme Court!

The Bible was once used as the standard of common sense, justice, and fairness, but we now live in a time when compromise is the norm. No longer are "right and wrong" guided by the biblical principle of right doing; now, the guiding question for many Americans has become, "Is it politically correct?" I don't know about you, but I am pretty sick and tired of *hearing the term p*olitical correctness from people in leadership positions! You may be asking what this term means, and let me answer you by stating that what I'm about to say may not be considered politically correct! I define political correctness as any instance where a person or committee with authority (such as elected government officials, civic leaders, or even church leaders) refuses to take a stand against others whose purpose is to compromise or destroy God's moral laws— laws that are the cornerstone of the Constitution of the United States *and* the Christian church.

Political correctness is playing a major role in reshaping the minds and values of America, sending us into a downward spiral of immorality and lawlessness. There is only one solution to this problem, and the Bible gives us the answer in John 8:32: "And you shall know the truth, and the truth shall make you free."

So what is truth? God established the Ten Commandments, which are the transcript of His own character and the foundation of His perfect government. He gave them to our sinful world to help guide us to right doing. The further we distance ourselves from God and His principles of life, the quicker our great nation will find itself in national ruin!

As a Christian, I believe I am saved by accepting the Lord Jesus Christ, who shed His blood on the Cross of Calvary as atonement for my sins. Our Lord said, "If you love Me, keep My commandments" (John 14:15), and the Apostle John further instructs us, "For this is the love of God, that we keep His commandments. And His commandments are not burdensome" 1 John 5:3. So, I believe the Ten Commandments are a gift from God to guide us to His abundant life.

A Great Spiritual Decline
It's reasonable to think that all Christians will stand in defense of God's commandments, yet the liberal media has

impacted many Christian churches in America, as well, effecting a great decline in true spirituality over the last four or five decades. Many church leaders are laboring to be politically correct, and no longer stand up for the Bible principles of good and evil, right and wrong. Why? Because their church members are so influenced by the secular world that they no longer tolerate some Bible truths.

I talked to a minister this past week who recently attended a conference of interfaith religious group leaders meeting in New York City. The Pastor told me that a number of those who were gathered there were gay and lesbian pastors and clergy. He also told me that prayer was never once a part of the conference, even when eating their food. Why? Because they didn't want to offend any of the attendees, though they were all church leaders!

Many mainstream Christian organizations and denominations have shifted their perspective on same-sex relationships. In 2015, the Presbyterian Church in America voted to redefine marriage as "a commitment between two people, traditionally a man and a woman." This modification to the church's constitution now allows for same-sex marriage. [2]

A 2009 resolution of the Evangelical Lutheran Church of America (ELCA) also allows same-sex couples to marry, but leaves it up to individual ministers to decide if they will marry them. But in 2012, ELCA Secretary David Swartling said, "There is nothing that prescribes who a congregation pastor can marry or not marry, so long as it is consistent with state law." [3]

The Episcopal Church has also joined the ranks of church organizations that allow same-sex marriage, as well as openly gay clergy. In 2012, they established a "rite of blessing" for same-sex couples, but didn't have an official denominational position on gay marriage. Then, in 2015, the bishops at the Episcopal General Convention authorized their clergy to

---

2 Time.com, "Three Other Christian Denominations That Allow Gay Marriage," http://time.com/3749253/churches-gay-marriage/ (accessed 5/15/17).
3 *Ibid.*

perform same-sex weddings, if they choose to do so, along with the right to refuse, if they so decide.[4]

Today, there are dozens of denominations and congregations around the world that are in support of same-sex marriage. They are considered "LGBT affirming."

Churches Affirming Abortion?

There are also varying stances on abortion within Christian denominations. The United Church of Christ, for example, holds a more liberal approach. In a 1971 position paper, it reaffirmed that the availability of safe and legal abortions is consistent with a woman's right to "follow the dictates of her own faith."

Since 1987, the Unitarian Universalist Association has espoused that a woman has the right to choose both contraception and abortion as an expression of her constitutional rights. They also support legislative funding of safe abortions for low-income women and oppose any denial of government funds restricting access to contraceptive and abortion services.

In addition, both the American Presbyterian Church and the Evangelical Lutheran Church in America are essentially pro-choice, as well.

Itching Ears

Where are God's commandments in all of this? The Bible describes this condition in 2 Timothy 4:3–4: "For the time will come when they will not endure sound doctrine, but according to their own desires, because they have itching ears, they will heap up for themselves teachers; and they will turn their ears away from the truth, and be turned aside to fables."

The pews of megachurches may be filled on Sunday mornings across America, but church attendance is not the measuring stick for true spirituality. When Jesus called the

---

4 http://amp.timeinc.net/time/3749253/churches-gay-marriage/?source=dam (accessed 5/15/17).

religious leaders of His day hypocrites, He quoted from the prophet Isaiah in Isaiah 29:13 saying, "These people draw near to Me with their mouth, and honor Me with their lips, but their heart is far from Me. And in vain they worship Me, teaching as doctrines the commandments of men" Matthew 15:8–9. Wow! This text should be a wake-up call to all of us Christians to get back to the Bible—and the Bible only—as our guide to eternal life.

The Ten Commandments were etched in stone by the very finger of God. Man can break God's Law, but he can never change it! Finite man cannot change something that is eternal. In America today, we're seeing our government—and even some churches—chipping away at the cornerstone that ensures that our society will live in peace and harmony, and the effects will end in disaster. When the cornerstone is removed from any building, it is only a matter of time before it collapses!

CHAPTER
III

WHAT IS A SPIRITUAL VIGILANTE?

The collapse of our society is not the will of most Americans. It is the result of groups and organizations with a mission to violate our moral laws for their own selfish purposes. However, they're smart enough to embrace some good causes in order to gain support for their morally corrupt agenda, and that's why I've entitled this book, *Spiritual Vigilantes*.

The legal dictionary section of thefreedictionary.com defines *vigilantism* as "Taking the law into one's own hands and attempting to effect justice according to one's own understanding of right and wrong . . . action taken by an individual or group to protest existing law; action taken by an individual or group to enforce a higher law than that enacted by society's designated lawmaking institutions; private enforcement of legal norms in the absence of an established, reliable, and effective law enforcement body." [5]

This explanation of a vigilante is the definition in *physical*

---

5 thefreedictionary.com, "Vigilantism," http://legal-dictionary.thefreedictionary.com/Vigilantism (accessed 5/15/17).

terminology; however, this book will examine what I call *spiritual* vigilantes—those who attempt to take God's Law into their own hands without any authority from Heaven to do so. Special interest groups, legislators, and even some church leaders have become spiritual vigilantes by taking God's Law and tossing out inspired restrictions, determining for themselves what is right and wrong.

As Christians, we live in the physical world, but we fight a spiritual battle every day. Ephesians 6:12 says it like this: "For we do not wrestle against flesh and blood, but against principalities, against powers, against the rulers of the darkness of this age, against spiritual hosts of wickedness in the heavenly places." There's a Great Controversy going on between Christ and Satan over the souls of men. Where will we spend eternity? Will we spend it in Heaven, or will we be separated from God forever?

Vigilantes use all kinds of excuses for taking the law into their own hands. They believe that the governing law that is in place is not sufficient, so they justify enforcing their own laws as a higher law of authority. Whether they protest the laws of the land, or the Law of God, the results are disastrous.

I believe America and the Christian Church are looking for men and women in leadership who will not be bought or sold, leaders who will stand for what's right at any cost! Many of our politicians do not have the courage to stand up to groups that are tearing down the moral fabric of this country.

The first four commandments describe man's duties and obligations to his Creator God, and the last six commandments outline man's duty to his fellow man. To protect the rights of all people, the Constitution of the United States includes the last six of the Ten Commandments given to us by God to allow us to live in a free and peaceful society.

Redefining Marriage

We all know that discrimination is a hot button in American politics, and rightfully so. Without going into great detail, there have been, and still are, some great injustices being done to people of color in America. And while great progress has been made—from slavery to President—it is our government's responsibility to ensure that all Americans have equal rights, not only for minorities, but for everyone. Democracy is why America is such a great nation. It is meant to work for everyone, and while we still have a long way to go, God's Ten Commandments play an important role in ensuring these rights for all Americans. Without them, we would not know right from wrong.

Our government leaders know that discrimination still exists, but there are some minority groups who use this platform of discrimination to rally their fellow Americans to trample on God's Law. The LGBTQ community is an example of a minority group that represents only an estimated three to five percent of the American population, yet they were able to champion their cause all the way to the Supreme Court. Same-sex marriage is now the law of the land, even though it is in direct opposition to God's Ten Commandment Law, adopted by our founding fathers as part of the Constitution of the United States of America. This didn't happen by a majority vote of the people of the United States. In fact, Americans never got to vote on the issue at all. Same-sex marriage was deemed a federal/constitutional case by the government, and that took it all the way to the Supreme Court, bypassing the will of local communities.

God said He created them male and female, and He blessed and sanctified their marriage to each other, saying, "Be fruitful and multiply." Genesis 1:22. Notice that God did not create Adam and Steve in the Garden of Eden. If this had been the case, you and I would not be alive today.

By redefining marriage, the Supreme Court became a

spiritual vigilante. Why do I say that? Because they overruled God's authority. While the Supreme Court is the highest court in the United States, sooner or later they will have to answer to a Higher Power—the almighty Creator God our forefathers wrote about. He instituted holy matrimony between one man and one woman during Creation Week in the Garden of Eden, and no earthly power has the authority to negate His blessed and sanctified institutions!

Many government and church leaders seem to have lost their backbones, and I believe the reason many of them won't take a stand is that they're afraid of offending the offenders! They do not want a head-on confrontation that will cause division among their constituents and a loss of votes for themselves. They're not willing to stand up for principle—a fundamental truth that serves as the foundation for a system of belief or behavior. However, nothing we build in life will last without a solid foundation.

The Foundation of Our Constitution

Our Founding Fathers wisely wrote the Constitution to make a legal separation between church and state. America was populated because millions of people had suffered through over 1,000 years of religious persecution from the Church of Rome. They fled the religious persecution of the "old country" for religious freedom in the new world. Although America is not officially a Christian nation, our Founding Fathers based much of our Constitution, as well as our state and federal laws on God's eternal moral law, The Ten Commandments.

Let me quote John Quincy Adams: "The law given from Sinai was a civil and municipal as well as a moral and religious code; it contained many statutes adapted to that time only, and to the particular circumstances of the nation to whom it was given; they could of course be binding upon them, and only upon them, until abrogated by the same authority which enacted them, as they afterward were by the Christian dispensation: but many others were of universal application—laws essential to the existence of men in society, and most of which have been enacted by every nation, which ever professed any code of laws."[6]

Noah Webster penned this: "The duties of men are summarily comprised in the Ten Commandments, consisting of two tables; one comprehending the duties which we owe immediately to God—the other, the duties we owe to our fellow men."[7]

He also said this in the preface to the 1828 edition of his *American Dictionary of the English Language:* "In my view, the Christian religion is the most important and one of the first things in which all children, under a free government ought to be instructed. . . . No truth is more evident to my mind than that the Christian religion must be the basis of any government intended to secure the rights and privileges of a free people."

When sin came into the world through the fall of Adam and Eve, God gave mankind a template, or set of principles to live by called the Ten Commandments, and since no society can live in peace and harmony without them, they have become the basis for the laws of the land in most of the countries of this world.

---

6 John Quincy Adams, *Letters of John Quincy Adams, to His Son, on the Bible and Its Teachings,* p. 61.
7 Noah Webster, *A Collection of Papers on Political, Literary, and Moral Subjects, by Noah Webster,* p. 296.

CHAPTER IV

THE LAST SIX COMMANDMENTS

I am amazed that so many people today do not acknowledge that the Ten Commandments are the foundation of our democratic society, even though our Founding Fathers acknowledged that these laws of God were timeless—a must for any civilized society to live by.

Let's read the last six commandments first, as these are the moral laws our Founding Fathers adopted when creating the United States Constitution. They were intended to protect and preserve the lives of its citizens. They are found in Exodus 20:12–17:

Fifth commandment: "Honor your father and your mother, that your days may be long upon the land which the Lord your God is giving you."

Sixth commandment: "You shall not murder."

Seventh commandment: "You shall not commit adultery."

Eighth commandment: "You shall not steal."

Ninth commandment: "You shall not bear false witness against your neighbor."

Tenth commandment: "You shall not covet your neighbor's house; you shall not covet your neighbor's wife, nor his male servant, nor his female servant, nor his ox, nor his donkey, nor anything that is your neighbor's."

I believe we can easily identify these six commandments as laws of the land that have been adopted by our United States government. They dictate our actions toward our fellow man, and the United States Supreme Court can enforce them on its citizens. However, the State cannot mandate its citizens to keep the first four commandments, and neither should they, because they are given to each of us by God and concern our relationship with our Creator. The cornerstone of God's Ten Commandments is found within the first four, because without it, we wouldn't know Who authored the other six.

Let's take a few examples of the State's adoption of the last six commandments, which pertain to our obligation to our fellow man:

Fifth Commandment: "Honor your father and your mother . . ." This commandment teaches young people that they are to honor and respect their father and mother. In turn, their parents' responsibility is to teach them to respect God, family, and country.

Here in America, parents are responsible for protecting and providing for the needs of their offspring until they are 18 years old. In return, children must be accountable to their parents for their actions, and if they choose to lead a life of crime or physically abuse their parents or others at any age before they turn 18, their custody will be awarded to the state courts, which will decide their punishment.

Sixth Commandment: "You shall not murder."
The murder of another human being is a crime against God and the laws of the State. Accused murderers will be tried in a court of law by their fellow citizens, and their fate will be decided by a judge, according to the laws of the Supreme Court. Abortion is taking the life of the unborn. Until the Roe v. Wade court case of 1973, abortion was considered murder, yet the Supreme Court has legalized most abortions. However, the killing of unborn babies is still a sin in the court of Heaven, which supersedes the United States Supreme Court!

Seventh Commandment: "You shall not commit adultery."
The word "adultery" includes any sexual relations outside of marriage. In Genesis 2:24, our Creator God made marriage a union between one man and one woman, and like other state laws related to sex, sodomy, fornication, and rape, adultery laws extend back to the Old Testament. Abundant Bible texts explicitly prohibit rape, incest, homosexuality, fornication, sodomy, bestiality, and the like in passages such as Leviticus 18:22 and 20:13; 1 Corinthians 6:9; 1 Timothy 1:9–10; Romans 1:26–27; and many others.

For nearly 200 years, adultery by either spouse was a crime in the United States. Having sex outside of one's marriage is considered adultery, and adultery laws have always included sodomy, homosexual relationships, incest, pedophilia, rape, etc. But while adultery is still a crime in some states, those laws are softening quickly, mainly due to the redefinition of marriage by the Supreme Court to include same-sex marriage. According to Wikipedia, in the United States, "Sexual activities with a person of the opposite sex as well as the same sex involving oral sex and other sexual behavior not necessarily including intercourse constitute adultery. In order to use adultery as grounds for a divorce, the filing party must present sufficient proof that the other party had sexual relations with a third party." [8]

---

8 https://en.wikipedia.org/wiki/Grounds_for_divorce_(United_States) - See Adultery subtitle (accessed 5/15/14).

Eighth Commandment: "You shall not steal."
Stealing, of course, is still against the law of the land, and a very important one for any civilization to live by, since abiding by it helps ensure peace and harmony.

Ninth Commandment: "You shall not bear false witness against your neighbor."
This commandment concerns a murder of a different kind. This is about character assassination against a fellow human being, something that is still against the laws of the State. Bearing false witness means willfully lying about someone to hurt or destroy their character for any reason. If convicted in a court of law, a jury will decide the person's fate, just as they do when one breaks any of the other laws of the land.

Tenth Commandment: "You shall not covet . . ."
Coveting becomes a crime when a person's lust or desire for something he/she doesn't possess, leads to acting on the lust. Coveting can be the cause of stealing, adultery, rape, bearing false witness, murder, etc.

Seals of Authority
What do these laws—the laws of God and the laws of the United States government—have in common, when transgressed by its citizens? Simply this: When we break any one of them, there's a penalty to be paid. We can term this as *accountability*. The lawbreaker is held accountable for his/her actions when he/she breaks the law.

But let's look at this a little closer: Any individual could write down these six commandments, but no one is likely to abide by them, unless they know that the author has full authority to hold him accountable for breaking or ignoring them, don't you agree?

The Constitution of the United States, written by our government's Founding Fathers, is the law of the land; and this law is enforced by the United States Supreme Court, the highest court in the land. The Supreme Court does not write the laws; it merely enforces them (the Constitution, Bill of Rights, Preamble, etc.).

The Supreme Court Seal marks its authority, and it contains a name or title (Supreme Court) and the domain of its authority (the United States of America). The highest individual office in America is that of the President of the United States, who also has a seal showing his authority. This seal contains his name (Donald Trump), his title (President), and his domain (the United States of America).

In the same way, the Ten Commandments have a seal that includes the Author's name, His title, and His domain. The Seal of God is found in the fourth commandment—the cornerstone of the Ten Commandments. Let's read it. Exodus 20:8-11 says, "Remember the Sabbath day, to keep it holy. Six days you shall labor and do all your work, but the seventh day is the Sabbath of the Lord your God. In it you shall do no work: you, nor your son, nor your daughter, nor your male servant, nor your female servant, nor your cattle, nor your stranger who is within your gates. For in six days the Lord made the heavens and the earth, the sea, and all that is in them, and rested the seventh day. Therefore the Lord blessed the Sabbath day and hallowed it."

This fourth commandment is the cornerstone because it contains the seal of the living God. What is that seal? Let's look at it: His name (Lord God), His title (Creator), and His domain (Heaven and Earth).

We see here that the Constitution of the United States and the Ten Commandments both have a seal of authority. The Constitution serves as the most important government document because it defines the laws of the land. In turn, these laws are enforced by the Supreme Court—the highest court in the land. However, the Ten Commandments, written on stone by the finger of God, have authority over all His creation in Heaven and Earth for eternity. Isn't it amazing that relatively small groups of organized people can influence an entire government to try to change God's moral laws and affect the entire population of a nation?

These groups of people, whose mission is to erase the line in the sand between right and wrong and good and evil, are not limited to the United States. This is a worldwide movement whose leader is none other than Satan, the father of lies! These people deny God or misrepresent Him while pushing their agenda to all who will listen.

CHAPTER V

THE SILENT MAJORITY

In my opinion, those who misrepresent God are much more dangerous to society than those who deny His existence. The reason this is dangerous is because many Christians are "carried about with every wind of doctrine" (Ephesians 4:14) due to their lack of knowledge and spiritual discernment. Christians who fail to take a stand against those who trample the moral and spiritual laws of God are just as responsible for a nation's rejection of God's laws as those who openly reject them!

The United States of America is a democracy, a government formed by the people and for the people, and ruled by a majority. For a Christian to be silent when there's an attack on the very foundation on which this country was built is not only shameful, but sinful as well! Silence by Christian people when a government takes God's Law into their own hands to destroy or redefine it is unacceptable to God!

I believe that the majority of Christians have played a major role in creating a politically-correct society! Why do I say this?

Because Christians are too often silent, instead of standing up against blatant sin by their government, civic organizations, and even church leaders. It seems as though the majority of Christians would rather remain silent than to hold their leaders accountable when laws are being passed that take away our religious liberties.

The devil doesn't care which side of the boat we fall out of, as long as we fall out. Political correctness is justified by many Christians because they don't want to offend anyone for being different from themselves. And do you know what? I agree with that . . . to a point. As Christians, we should not be in the business of offending people just because they come from a different religious, cultural, or ethnic background from our own. Jesus is our example, and He loves everyone. John 15:9–10 says, "As the Father loved Me, I also have loved you; abide in My love. If you keep My commandments, you will abide in My love, just as I have kept My Father's commandments and abide in His love."

The mission of every Christian should be to love everyone, no matter how much we disagree with them. We don't have a right to judge others, since we are all sinners saved by grace (see Matthew 7:1). So how people choose to live their lives is their choice, right? I would answer that question by saying, "Yes—as long as it doesn't affect or take away the rights of someone else."

However, this is not what's happening today in our great country. Religious liberty, along with other rights, is being taken away from our citizens at an alarming rate. Christians should not be silent when it comes to protecting our Constitution and our religious liberty. *We need to be heard by our civic, state, and federal government leaders.*

Right Is Wrong and Wrong Is Right
Liberal media has played an enormous role in encouraging people to believe that right is wrong and wrong is right, and

the impact of media on all our lives cannot be overstated! Television, radio, newspapers, and social media influence us every day like never before in Earth's history, and yes, they are working hard to erase the line in the sand between male and female, as created by God!

The goal of liberal media and our government's public school system is to indoctrinate our young children as they grow up in a social environment where there are no lines in the sand between right and wrong, or between genders. But to deny the gender difference between male and female is to deny the existence of a Creator God!

Another social and spiritual line in the sand is in the abortion arena. Legalized abortion was the first major step taken by the United States government to chip away at the Ten Commandment Law of God. The abortion law is still a point of contention and division in the United States.

As followers of Christ, there are steps we can, and should take, to uphold the "You shall not murder" commandment. Those who vote for candidates that support and champion "Pro-Choice" abortion groups should ask themselves whether or not, in the courts of Heaven, they are accessories to murder. Over 60,000,000 unborn babies have been murdered since Roe v. Wade became the law of the land in 1973!

There may not be degrees of murder, but wouldn't you agree with me that murder against the most defenseless human beings in our society—the unborn—seems especially atrocious? I would challenge each reader to research Margaret Sanger, the founder of Planned Parenthood. She wrote, "Consequences of breeding from stock lacking human vitality always will give us social problems and perpetuate institutions of charity and crime." [9] Her mission for Planned Parenthood was not really just for all women to have a choice whether or not to have an abortion. It appears to be aimed at the government deciding who should live and who should die!

---

9 Margaret Sanger, *Causes Back of Social Programs*, Typed Draft. Source: Margaret Sanger Papers, Sophia Smith Collection, Margaret Sanger Microfilm S73:0029. https://www.nyu.edu/projects/sanger/webedition/app/documents/show.php?sangerDoc=236398.xml (accessed 5/15/17).

Her statements were "code" aimed at reducing the black population in the early 1900s.

I am very much aware that there are times when medically-induced abortions may be the right choice when it comes to saving the life of the mother, or in a variety of emergency situations. However, barring one of these medical necessities, killing a baby is unconscionable.

Consider this: Why is it illegal to kill the baby five minutes after delivery, but legal, in some states, to kill him/her five minutes *before* delivery? When I talk to fellow Christians about this subject, it seems I get a patented answer: "Well, I don't support abortion, but I think this candidate is better than the opposing one on many other issues."

Would you vote for the candidate of your choice if he/she accidentally ran over and killed a small child riding a tricycle in the street? My guess is, you would still vote for him/her, because it was an accident. It would not affect your opinion of the candidate or his/her campaign agenda.

But what if you find out that the candidate of your choice ran over that small child with the intention of killing him/her? I would guess that the other issues they campaigned on would now be insignificant compared to purposely killing a defenseless child! I think I can safely say that you would not disregard the fact that he/she killed an innocent child because you like his/her other political positions.

So my point is this: Abortion is taking the life of a real human being. According to the sixth commandment, this is murder.

Let me use another example. You see a murder about to happen, but you don't do anything about it, even though it could be proven in court that you had an opportunity to intervene, or at least call 911. Would you be an accessory to that murder?

Or, let's say that you not only witnessed a murder of another human being, but you actually handed the attacker the blunt instrument to make it happen. Should you be charged as an accessory to the crime? As straightforward as this may sound, don't you think the consequences would be the same when you vote for someone who supports and champions abortions? In other words, when you vote for a candidate who supports killing the most vulnerable human beings in our society, will the Lord hold you accountable as being an accessory to these murders because you not only didn't do anything to prevent them from happening, but instead supported the murderer?

I realize that my stance on this subject will be deemed divisive by some, but I would rather err on the side of mercy and rightdoing when I stand before God on Judgment Day. How about you?

When a Christian stands up to voice his objections to the government's role in redefining marriage, its encouragement of young people in public schools to experiment with homosexual relationships, or to cry out against the abortion of the most helpless people in our society, he's quickly accused of discriminating against those he disagrees with. Wrong becomes right, and right becomes wrong, according to media bias. The media will blast anyone who opposes what the Bible defines as sin, but there's an old saying that says, "If we don't stand for something, we'll fall for anything!"

Between a Rock and a Hard Place

In case you're not sure what sin is, let's allow Scripture to define it. In 1 John 3:4, the Bible says, "Whosoever committeth sin transgresseth also the law: for sin is the transgression of the law." Here the Bible clearly tells us that breaking or transgressing the Ten Commandment Law of God is the definition of sin.

I rarely hear our government and civic leaders encourage Americans to place God, family, and country first, as they did when I was growing up. Why? Because it's no longer politically expedient for many of them. Too often, truth has been sold out to political correctness! We are living in a society where very little value is placed on God, family, and country. The sad truth is that not only do our government leaders bow in political correctness to a minority of the people, but so do many of our church leaders and Christians, both here in America and around the world!

You need to know that because I don't want to be in a position of compromise, I'm neither a registered Republican nor a Democrat. Personally speaking, I don't join any political party because when I do, I am connecting myself to their particular platform. I believe that I'm in a better position to be objective if I'm not formally tied to either party, and I don't know about you, but I have yet to see a political party I can align myself with in good conscience.

And while I think I should be vocal and stand for right against government actions that try to change or negate God's Law, the answer is not in committing myself to a political party, but in committing myself to Jesus Christ.

An Example

Political correctness, in many cases, is nothing more than compromising principles of truth with error. Politicians will often change their position on certain issues, thinking that it might give them an advantage over the opponent—even if the flip-flop goes against the principles of truth they've held dear for many years.

Let me try to apply this political correctness term with an example. The Bible is very clear on the subject of homosexuality, and while I'm not going to go into an in-depth study on this sin, here are a few Bible texts you can look up on your own: Leviticus 18:22; Romans 1:26–28; Jude 5–8; 1 Timothy 1:8–11; and 1 Corinthians 6:9–11 and 7:2.

People have been living homosexual lifestyles for thousands of years, but in most cases, they've lived as "closeted" homosexuals. This term simply means that most of them know that the lifestyle they are living is against God's moral law and the law of the land. In the past, many have kept their affairs secret for fear that "straight" people might play God, judge them for their open sin, and seek to physically hurt them or destroy their reputations.

Homosexual Americans now have the same rights as anyone else under our Constitution, including same-sex marriage. No one can or should be targeted or bullied by vigilante groups because of their sexual preference, according to our laws. Although same-sex marriage is an abomination in the sight of God, it is now the law of the land; but rebellion against God and His law comes at a price.

The fine line our politicians have to deal with is that the gay community not only wants equal rights, but also wants rights that take away from the majority of other American's rights! Transgender public bathroom freedom is one example. If local and federal governments support it, this "freedom" will take away the rights of the majority of other Americans who are overwhelmingly against such a law. Once the stone is rolling down the hill, it becomes very hard to stop!

The LGBTQ community was able to gain the support of the National Association for the Advancement of Colored People (NAACP) and other civil rights leaders and organizations across our nation, and this now gives them a much broader platform and a much louder voice to be heard by our politicians. Rejection of any part of their platform can now be perceived as equal to the rejection of Black America's civil rights. Talk about a fine line for politicians to walk!

This is where political correctness rears its ugly head. Government leaders are between the proverbial rock and a hard place, so rather than take a stand on what's right and wrong, they tend to go along with this community—even when it tramples on the rights of other Americans.

CHAPTER
VI

HOW IT HAPPENED

You may be asking the same question I asked: How did the homosexual community get the support of the NAACP and the federal government?

The answer is simply that the LGBTQ community was able to garner NAACP support by proclaiming that their civil rights were being violated, since the laws of the land interfered with their desire for marriage equality. For hundreds of years, same-sex marriage was not legal because it was in violation of God's moral law, as adopted by our government. Same-sex marriage would be a violation of the seventh commandment, "You shall not commit adultery." But some in minority communities identify with the marginalization of the gay community, empathizing with them. And this is important: By receiving support from the NAACP and others in the minority community, the LGBTQ community was able to move their disregard for God's Law and law of the land from a *moral issue* to a *civil rights* issue!

I'm all for civil rights, but the LGBTQ community *does not* qualify for civil rights protection because of their sexual preference. Why? Because being born with homosexual tendencies cannot be equally compared to a person who is born black. Let me explain. A homosexual, who is a Christian, for instance, makes the choice whether or not he is going to follow his "unnatural" desires, as the Bible terms it, by acting on his desire to lie with his fellow man, or to follow God's Word and be celibate. The key word here is *choice!* None of us can choose our nationality, gender, or color at birth!

Let's examine this a little further. Many young children are born alcoholics through their parents. Yet, when they are old enough to drive, the law does not allow them to claim that their civil rights are being violated when they get arrested for drunk driving. Why? Even though they may have been born alcoholics, they still chose to break the law by driving intoxicated!

Same-sex marriage is a violation of God's moral law, as found in the seventh commandment. Adultery is also a violation of the moral law. This abrogation of God's moral law cannot be excused as a violation of anyone's civil rights. The Bible terms such action as sin—a conscious rebellion against God's laws—and therefore, a choice.

Though we are born with a sinful nature, we still can choose between loving God and keeping His commandments, or rebelling against His physical and spiritual laws! When we choose to violate God's laws, we cannot claim that our civil rights are being violated because we are only doing what comes natural to us.

As I read the Bible, I come to the conclusion that no one will be denied entry to Heaven because of the color of their skin, or their physical gender at birth. However, same-sex marriage, adultery, incest, rape, murder, stealing, lying, coveting, etc., are all sins that are choices!

The Bible promises that, "If we confess our sins, He is

faithful and just to forgive us our sins and to cleanse us from all unrighteousness" 1 John 1:9. But *commandment rebellion,* as I call it, is different from falling into temptation and committing a sin, followed by repentance and asking God's forgiveness. Commandment rebellion is when a person chooses to live a lifestyle of rebellion against any of God's commandments, and defends that lifestyle, even when it's a direct violation of His Ten Commandment Law. Romans 3:23 says, "For all have sinned and fall short of the glory of God," but to live in an unsanctified marriage, whether it be same-sex or heterosexual adultery, is to continue to rebel against God's law.

The fact that the United States Supreme Court ruled same-sex marriage to be legal does not change the fact that it is still sin. The fact that the United States Supreme Court ruled abortion to be legal does not negate the fact that it is still murder, according to God's Ten Commandments.

The Bible says that if we make a mistake, or fall into sin, we must confess that sin to Jesus, telling Him that we are sorry. But there is no forgiveness of sin without repentance! I want to make this really clear: *God hates sin, but loves the sinner! There is no sin He will not forgive.*

The Silence of Millions

I don't think anyone is denying that some LGBTQ people are born with a desire for same-sex relationships. My point is that being "gay" is a *moral* issue, not a *civil rights* issue. Not that many years ago, American law violated every Black American's civil rights when it designated "white" and "colored" bathrooms. This was a clear violation of Black American's civil rights! However, people who calls themselves transgender should not be able to use the public bathroom of their choice, depending on whether they *feel* they are a man or a woman on that particular day. This is utterly ridiculous and wrong! Disapproval by the majority of people and the local or federal government is not a rejection of that person's civil rights. In fact, in this case, it would be protecting the rights of the vast majority of Americans.

I'm very sure that the majority of Americans do not want transgender people in the bathrooms with their sons or daughters. The fear that this may open the doors for sexual predators to gain access to their children is a real concern to many.

I would dare to say that at least 80 to 90 percent of all Americans would agree, but politicians will not take a stance on such a no-brainer decision as this, because they don't want to be accused of discrimination against this minority group. They're much more concerned about being politically correct than they are about taking a stand for what's right!

Only a few years ago, both Barack Obama and Hillary Clinton publicly stated that they believed that marriage between one man and one woman should be upheld as the law of the land—as it has been from the inception of our Constitution. This is the biblical view of marriage that they both supported, and you can watch these interviews on YouTube.

But, as the LGBTQ community began to organize into a formidable organization, gaining the support of the NAACP by tying same-sex marriage to civil rights, some of our politicians began to waffle on their stance.

As the liberal media began to push for what was termed as "marriage equality," support for same-sex marriage continued to grow to the point that Barack Obama and Hillary Clinton did a total about-face and became great champions of same-sex marriage.

Soon, many other Bible-thumping politicians also began championing same-sex marriage, and, as you know, under the leadership of President Obama, same-sex marriage became the law of the land!

According to political fact-checking website, *politifact.com*,

"In August 2008, President Obama told Southern California megachurch Pastor Rick Warren his definition of marriage: 'I believe that marriage is the union between a man and a woman. Now, for me as a Christian, it is also a sacred union. God's in the mix.'"[10] However, only four years later, when *Good Morning America* host Robin Roberts asked him if he was still opposed to same-sex marriage, he answered, "At a certain point, I've just concluded that for me, personally, it is important for me to go ahead and affirm that I think same-sex couples should be able to get married."[11]

By Barack Obama's own statement, we can conclude that he consciously took God "out of the mix" in 2012! What happened to the sanctity of marriage? Politics kicked in!

Again we go to *politifact.com*: "[Hillary] Clinton came out in support of same-sex marriage in 2013 after more than a decade of opposing it." However, you may remember that her views really came to the spotlight when she became a presidential candidate in 2015. Politifact.com goes on to say, "We decided to put Clinton's statements about same-sex marriage on our Flip-O-Meter, which measures whether a candidate has changed their views without making a value judgment about such flips. We found that as public opinion shifted toward support for same-sex marriage, so did Clinton. She has had plenty of company among members of her own party to change their stance on same-sex marriage. In 2012, we gave Obama a Full Flop when he announced his support for same-sex marriage."[12]

Even a secular website like politifact.com reveals that Mr. Obama and Mrs. Clinton changed their opinion, or "flip-flopped," on same-sex marriage—not based on values, but on political pressure! Both politicians threw out God's Law to appease the demands of the LGBTQ community, even

---

10 Politifact.com, "President Barack Obama's Shifting Stance on Gay Marriage," http://www.politifact.com/truth-o-meter/statements/2012/may/11/barack-obama/president-barack-obamas-shift-gay-marriage/ (accessed 5/15/17).
11 *Ibid.*
12 Politifact.com, "Hillary Clinton's Changing Position on Same-Sex Marriage," http://www.politifact.com/truth-o-meter/statements/2015/jun/17/hillary-clinton/hillary-clinton-change-position-same-sex-marriage/ (accessed 5/15/'7).

though the percentage of gay people is estimated at only three to five percent of the American population.

"How could this have happened," you might ask, "when such a small amount of the people in the United States were in support of redefining marriage?" What went wrong was the *silence* of millions of Christian people. Their silence was a vote for same-sex marriage.

Many politicians are smart. They knew that the LGBTQ community had the support of many civil rights leaders, as well as Hollywood, the NFL, the progressive left, and social media groups—not to mention the liberal media. Obama and Clinton would not turn a deaf ear to those who helped Mr. Obama gain the White House!

Those politicians also banked on the fact that millions of Christians who were against same-sex marriage would not take a public stand against it, and history proves their gamble paid off for them, and their party, in securing the Presidency of the United States for Barack Obama!

To maintain job security, these politicians willfully and knowingly trampled on our Creator God's first two blessed, sanctified, and holy institutions: marriage and the seventh-day Sabbath. We'll talk more about this later on.

Mandated Morality Doesn't Work

Some of you may rightfully say that there have always been people both here in the United States and around the world who don't live by the Ten Commandments. Sure, there have always been homosexuals living together; but the big difference is that this lifestyle was never sanctioned or adopted as a law of the government.

There's a big difference between the rejection of God's moral law by an individual, as opposed to its rejection by the government. Why? Because our democracy is set up to be controlled by the majority of people. When we as Christians are silent on issues such as same-sex marriage, for instance, lawmakers are not held accountable. The groups who are promoting their agendas override the silent Christians. And why not? The liberal media has done such an effective job of attacking those who oppose same-sex marriage that it almost makes Christian opposition seem un-Christian! Right seems wrong and wrong seems right.

Separation of Church and State

All that said, I don't agree with some of the organizations that support electing a majority of Christians into public office so they can *mandate* laws that will force Christianity on the rest of their fellow Americans. I believe that individuals should have the right to worship God—or not—without interference from the government, unless their actions break the laws adopted from the last six commandments of the original Ten Commandments. What do I mean by this? Simply that God gave us His Ten Commandments to help preserve and protect us from each other. No government can exist for long without laws to protect and defend the rights and lives of its people.

The Judeo-Christian theme in America's governance cannot be denied, though many may try. There's no doubt that our Founding Fathers believed in a Creator God who gave us a management system they adopted as part of their own. We all can read the theme of our monetary system—every dollar bill and every coin is engraved with the line, "In God We Trust."

Our Constitution's firm position on the separation of Church and State is in place to ensure religious liberty for its people, and I believe our Founding Fathers were led by God to include it in this important document!

The State has no control over how and when an individual chooses to worship their God or gods; and the Church can't control our government as it did during the Dark Ages when the Roman Catholic Church reigned supreme for hundreds of years, leading to the torture and murder of millions upon millions without government intervention!

Today we see a movement from the progressive left that undermines the commandments of God on both murder (abortion) and adultery (same-sex marriage). Then, on the right, we see a movement by many evangelicals to gain control of government by electing Christian politicians to enact religious laws that will take away certain religious liberties from every citizen.

It is no secret that religious organizations dating back to the late 1970s, including Jerry Falwell's Moral Majority, were formed with the purpose of tearing down the wall of separation between Church and State in the name of religion.

"The origins of the Moral Majority can be traced to 1976 when Baptist minister Jerry Falwell embarked on a series of 'I Love America' rallies across the country to raise awareness of social issues important to him," says *wikipedia.org.* "These rallies were an extension of Falwell's decision to go against the traditional Baptist principle of separating religion and politics, a change of heart Falwell said he had when he perceived what he described as the decay of the nation's morality." [13]

"Christian right or religious right is a term used mainly in the United States to label right-wing Christian political factions that are characterized by their strong support of socially conservative policies. Christian conservatives principally seek to apply their understanding of the teachings of Christianity to politics and public policy by proclaiming the value of those teachings or by seeking to use those teachings to influence law and public policy." [14]

Neither the progressive left nor the religious right should be allowed to influence the Supreme Court to mandate self-serving laws that violate the rights of its citizens! The liberal

---

13 Wikipedia.org, "Moral Majority," https://en.wikipedia.org/wiki/Moral_Majority (accessed 5/15/17).
14 Wikipedia.org, "Christian Right," https://en.wikipedia.org/wiki/Christian_right (accessed 5/15/17).

left will not stop until their mission to remove any evidence that God exists in the United States of America is completed. On the other hand, if the religious right has their way, they will tear down the separation between Church and State.

Many of the evangelicals from the Moral Majority in the past—and more recently, from the Christian right—believe that the United States should enact a National Sunday Law as a day of rest. This bill would require businesses to close on Sunday, in honor of the idea that Sunday is a traditional day of rest. Many believe that, by enacting this law, God will bless the United States of America. Why? Because it will signify to Him and the world that America is, once again, a Christian nation, and that its citizens are required to "rest" on this day.

When this happens, the wall of separation between Church and State will have fallen. Without the support of our Constitution, American citizens' religious freedom will be lost, just as it has been during the downfall of many governments, even in recent history.

In the next chapter, I will give some examples of countries that have trampled God's moral laws, and "kicked Him out" of their nation.

CHAPTER
VII

NATIONAL RUIN WITHOUT GOD

As you can see, our nation's Constitution has been under attack from both sides of the aisle for many years. But what has changed in the last two or three decades in America is that politicians, and sometimes church leaders, will not stand up against organized groups of people who defy God's Law, and the law of the land.

We live in the age of social media, and one doesn't have to own a television or radio station, or even a newspaper, to have enough influence to grab the ear of the politicians. Social media groups have become every bit as effective at pressuring politicians today as some of the special interest or lobbyist groups. But while it's great to be living in an age of the Web, it has also had its negative effects as well.

We've always had politicians who compromise their beliefs on certain issues to gain votes, and we've had our share of politicians who bow to pressure from big money players, gangsters, worker unions, and special interest and lobbyist groups. Since our government was first formed, people have successfully used sex, money, and power to influence individual politicians to allow themselves to become pawns of the rich and powerful.

But what we see today is unprecedented, and there's a reason for this. It goes back to the lines in the sand being swept away by the tide. The more politically correct a government (or a church, for that matter) becomes, the further it moves away from God's Laws. And the more any government moves away from God and His Laws, the sooner the nation ends up in ruins!

Ultimately, when a nation or church fails to uphold the Law of God as the standard for living in peace and harmony, evil will take control, as it did before the Flood. "Then the Lord saw that the wickedness of man was great in the earth, and that every intent of the thoughts of his heart was only evil continually" Genesis 6:5.

Taking Control
Let's take a look back into the not-so-distant history and see if there are any patterns that confirm that when a government turns from God, it ends up doing evil continually, resulting in national ruin.

Have you ever wondered how governments took control and how dictators such as Germany's Adolph Hitler, the USSR's Joseph Stalin, Cambodia's Pol Pot, or Cuba's Fidel Castro come into power? Is it possible that the United States could ever head down this kind of disastrous road? We can learn a lot from history, but I'll try to give a brief answer to this very complex question.

Countries that gain control of their people do it by deceit, and the dictionary defines *deceit* as "The act or practice of deceiving; concealment or distortion of the truth for the purpose of misleading; duplicity; fraud; cheating: an act or device intended to deceive." [15]

---

15 Dictionary.com, "Deceit," http://www.dictionary.com/browse/deceit?s=t (accessed 5/15/17).

This is happening in the United States already. Our government is allowing the moral law of God—the cornerstone or standard upon which our Constitution is built—to be done away with, and history records over and over how deceit and deception gain a foothold to take over the governments of free societies.

It usually starts when a country suffers a great economic depression, and soon communist leaders like those mentioned above begin to appear and campaign on fairness to all people—or in other words, on socialism. They campaign on "change," and when people are fighting to survive, they will "grab at a straw," as the old saying goes.

In Communist ideology, *the government* is God! Communism sees religion and God as enemies of the State. It says to its people, "We will take care of you," and this, of course, ends up in big government. The people are given free education, welfare, federal housing, etc., but all of this comes at a price! It comes at the cost of freedom. Taxes are raised exponentially. In Germany, for instance, when socialism took over, income taxes were raised from four percent to 60 percent!

It's an almost predictable series of events: The government claims property from its inhabitants, so the people become entirely dependent on it. When this happens, the citizens lose their independence. They become the property of the State, and can be treated as slaves, as Adolf Hitler, Pol Pot, Nicolae Ceausescu, Joseph Stalin, Mao Zedong, and many other leaders have proven. Stalin not only raised taxes, but also raised the mandatory weekly work hours. This turned the workforce into slave labor, just as Pol Pot did later on, in the 1970s.

Each of these countries went from socialism to communism. They bypassed their Constitutions by passing emergency law and order. Then they took control of the government and declared it a Communist State.

How National Ruin Begins

As we mentioned above, governments don't start out with dictators taking away all their citizens' freedoms, rights, and property. They go through stages. And that's why I think a look at history may help us see into the near future of the United States of America if we continue to negate God's moral laws as a nation. The Bible says, "Do not be deceived, God is not mocked; for whatever a man sows, that he will also reap" Galatians 6:7.

I've been to all of the countries I've mentioned, and I've seen the results of national ruin from governments whose leaders denounced God. When a government takes away the religious liberty of its citizens, it is an open statement that it views God as an enemy of the State. They know that where religious freedom is allowed, they will never have complete control of the people! But men were created to serve and worship God—not each other. Communist countries, and countries controlled by dictators, demand that their citizens give them loyalty and pay homage to government leaders— but *not* to the Creator God of Heaven.

Cambodia's Collapse

Without God and His moral law, human atrocities occur. I've visited Phnom Penh, Cambodia, and I've seen the Killing Fields firsthand. In the mid-to-late 1970s, while trying to start an agrarian utopia, Pol Pot killed between 1.5 and 2 million of his own people. He was inspired in part by Mao Zedong's Cultural Revolution, which he had witnessed firsthand during a visit to Communist China.

Anyone accused of having any allegiance to God, or anyone but Pol Pot, became an enemy of the State. Thousands of men, women, and children were detained and tortured at the infamous S–21, a detention center/prison (now the Tuol Sleng Museum). Pol Pot used barbarian forms of torture on his people–including cutting their fingers off one at a time, and other egregious acts I don't even want to mention here. From the detention center, the prisoners were taken to another location.

Pol Pot's soldiers had his prisoners dig miles of trenches, then made them stand in line by the thousands. Some of the them were given hammers and ordered to kill the person next to them, causing the victims to fall into their newly dug grave. If they refused, they would be tortured and killed themselves. Many times it was one of their own family members they were asked to kill. So, rather than see their friends and family tortured, their loved ones would commit the act, and then wait for their turn to be killed. The purpose of this barbaric mode of killing was simply to save bullets!

The bodies of these poor people who were so brutally murdered were exhumed, and over 8,000 skulls were put on display. The Killing Fields of Cheung Ek has a glass building housing the skulls. I stood in that very building and personally saw them, as well as the torture tools used to mutilate them. I can never forget what I witnessed in the Killing Fields!

Romania's Ruin

I was in Bucharest, Romania, shortly after dictator Ceausescu had been shot and killed, and his communist government overthrown. He hated church architecture so much that he destroyed at least 18 churches in that city. He also imprisoned many Protestant and evangelical church leaders during his reign. Local officials told me that some of the church leaders had refused to leave their office, so the government released a number of Gypsy prisoners who killed some of the pastors and their wives.

I visited a tent church, where members continued to come and worship even in the coldest winter weather after their church was torn down by this anti-God government. I also interviewed an old man, who at that time was a new Christian. He said he was an editor for the communist paper in the country for many years, and that he continuously ran stories that attempted to destroy the people's faith in God. He told me that most husbands and wives would not even discuss whether they believed in God with each other, because often, one of the spouses would inform the government, and the other would be sent to prison or killed. Why would they do such a thing? For a number of reasons I'm sure, but mainly because the government would not tolerate any disloyalty or any disrespect. Fearing the government might find out and hold both spouses accountable, many would become informants against their own family members. Neighbor would turn against neighbor because an informant might get a few extra rations of food for his family that week.

Massive Murders
I've heard the same types of stories in other Communist and former-Communist countries I've visited, such as Russia, Germany, China, and Cuba. I've interviewed many people about their government's oppression and the killings of many thousands of Christians because they refused to denounce their faith in their Creator God!

Stalin is estimated to have killed more than 20 million of his own countrymen in Russia; Hitler's Holocaust killed an estimated 6 million Jews, and close to another 5 million non-Jews, for a total of about 11 million; and Mao Zedong became the worst dictator mass murderer in history, killing over 45 million Chinese people! These people were worked, starved, or beaten to death during what was called, "The Great Leap Forward," over a period of just four years!

These governments hated religious freedom because they knew that Christians would be loyal to their God. Hundreds of dictators through the centuries have tried to stamp out individual's rights to serve God above man, and in the end, they've all failed. Millions of people have been persecuted and killed—not only at the hands of dictators, but also by those who claim to be agents of God. Yet the fire of Christianity can't be put out, because man can't extinguish what God establishes. His purposes will not be thwarted, and His word will not return to Him void.

The Very Worst Record

Despite the horrific killing history of Communist dictators, the worst record of killings the world has ever seen did not come from any of them. The most mass murders the world has ever seen came at the hands of a church!

During the Dark Ages (476–800 A.D.), millions of Christians were persecuted and killed at the hands of the Catholic Church in the name of religion! In fact, more people have been killed in religious wars than all the other wars combined! The best estimates indicate that anywhere from 50 to over 75 million people were killed by Papal Rome during the Catholic Inquisition alone—in the name of religion! [16] Why? Because the Church of Rome demanded that man's allegiance be given to the Church, rather than to God, as described in the first four of His Ten Commandments.

---

16 For more information see David Plaisted's 2006 paper, "Estimate of the Number Killed by the Papacy in the Middle Ages and Later," http://www.cs.unc.edu/~plaisted/estimates.html (accessed 5/15/17).

CHAPTER VIII

MAN'S DUTY TO GOD

L et's read the first four commandments to get a better understanding of why political systems, and even some religious leaders, hate them so much.

They are found in Exodus 20:1–11:

Commandment I: "And God spoke all these words, saying: "I am the Lord your God, who brought you out of the land of Egypt, out of the house of bondage. You shall have no other gods before Me."

Commandment II: "You shall not make for yourself a carved image—any likeness of anything that is in heaven above, or that is in the earth beneath, or that is in the water under the earth; you shall not bow down to them nor serve them. For I, the Lord your God, am a jealous God, visiting the iniquity of the fathers upon the children to the third and fourth generations of those who hate Me, but showing mercy to thousands, to those who love Me and keep My commandments."

Commandment III: "You shall not take the name of the Lord your God in vain, for the Lord will not hold him guiltless who takes His name in vain."

Commandment IV: "Remember the Sabbath day, to keep it holy. Six days you shall labor and do all your work, but the seventh day is the Sabbath of the Lord your God. In it you shall do no work: you, nor your son, nor your daughter, nor your male servant, nor your female servant, nor your cattle, nor your stranger who is within your gates. For in six days the Lord made the heavens and the earth, the sea, and all that is in them, and rested the seventh day. Therefore the Lord blessed the Sabbath day and hallowed it."

These first four commandments show man's duty to God. They remind us that we are all created by God and that our commitment to Him can only be shown by our actions. In other words, we must place our service and commitment to God before any earthly power.

Power-hungry regimes and many earthly governments—including some religions and cult leaders—demand man's allegiance to themselves. But God says, "You shall have no other gods before Me" in the *very first* commandment!

Our Duty to Man and to God

What, then, should be man's responsibility to his government? Jesus answered this when He told the Pharisees who questioned Him about paying taxes to Caesar: "Render therefore to Caesar the things that are Caesar's, and to God the things that are God's" Matthew 22:21. In other words, serve the government, work hard, pay taxes, and obey the laws of the land—as long as they don't conflict with the laws of God!

The law of the land is a physical law that only lasts for one's lifetime. However, the Law of God is spiritual, and lasts for eternity!

Remember, our duty to God is to . . .
1. have no other gods before Him.
2. not make any graven images and bow down to them.
3. not take the Lord's name in vain.
4. remember the Sabbath to keep it holy.

Now, for some reason, many church leaders "forget" about the fourth commandment. They teach that God only requires man to keep the other nine. But wouldn't you agree that as Christians we should keep *all* Ten Commandments, since they are all God's commandments, and not our own?

Let me ask you a question. If God intended for the fourth commandment to be done away with at the cross, would He have started it with "Remember" as the *first word?*

I think sometimes it's okay to use common sense when reading the Bible, don't you? So I have a question for husbands: Have you ever had your wife ask you to stop by the store on your way home from work and buy a loaf of bread, or a dozen eggs? When asking, has she ever said to you, "Remember—don't forget to stop by the store!" as you walked out the door?

For most of us guys, I'm sure that the answer is yes, and if she asks in this way, what does it tell you? I think it tells you that she knows you've been guilty of forgetting sometime in the past. She says, "Remember," because she's concerned you will forget.

Along the same line, the Lord must have known that we would forget to keep His Sabbath day holy, or else why would He have bothered to start the fourth commandment out with the word, "Remember"?

An all-knowing God knew that in time, mankind would forget to cease from his labors on the holy Sabbath, thereby abandoning his relationship with his Creator on this blessed and sanctified day. When God sanctified the seventh-day Sabbath, He set it apart. He made it a day of consecration, and He made it holy. We just read this in the fourth commandment.

I'm amazed at pastors who say that it doesn't make any difference which day you keep, as long as you keep one in seven. *The whole point is about allegiance and obedience to God.* Whom will we worship? The Creator God of the Universe? Or Satan, the father of lies?

I have another question for you husbands: Let's say you go to prayer meeting at church and there are seven men there, and when church is over, your wife announces to you that she is going home to stay the night with one of these men. Would that sit well with you? I'm sure you'd tell her that she can't do that *because marriage is sacred,* right? After all, God sanctified and made marriage a holy union between one man and one woman. But what if she responds that she doesn't think it makes any difference which man she picks of the seven, as long as she goes home with one of them?

I think you will agree that this situation is not likely to happen, because, as a Christian, she knows that there is only one man that God approves of her spending the night with, and that is her husband.

So let's re-emphasize that during Creation Week, God only made and sanctified two institutions: marriage between one man and one woman, and the seventh-day Sabbath. *We can no more substitute any other day of the week for the seventh-day Sabbath than substitute another spouse to join in our marriage.*

I've talked to many Christians, including pastors, who say they keep every day holy, but of course, that would be impossible to do since the Lord says we are to *work* six days a week and rest on the seventh-day Sabbath (Saturday). Also, we cannot keep a day holy that isn't holy in the first place. Only one day a week has been sanctified by God as His holy day—and that's the seventh day.

As we all know, the Bible records that God gave Moses

Ten Commandments for His people to live by. He did not give eight or nine commandments. God handed Moses two tables of stone on which He had engraved the Ten Commandments with His own finger.

So far, it seems very clear what day God made holy and how He instructed us to keep it. How ironic that 2,000 years later, the only commandment most Christians have forgotten is the only one that begins with the word "Remember."

It's Not Just About a Day

I want to emphasize here and now that we're going to find out that this whole Sabbath question is much bigger than a day. It's not just a Saturday versus Sunday issue. God could have chosen to sanctify and bless any other day of the week.

I like to think of it like this: We cannot really give God anything except our love and obedience. As our Creator, He already knows this, so that is all He asks of us. He says in John 14:15, "If you love Me, keep My commandments," so in order for us to show God we love Him, we must obey Him.

Men, you can tell your wife you love her, but if you never show her by your actions, she will eventually figure out that you really don't. There are certain things a man should remember to do to show his wife he loves her. For example, he should remember special days, such as her birthday, their anniversary, etc., and honor their love through his actions.

The same principle holds true in our relationship with God. He set aside the seventh day of the week to commune with His children through holy convocation. He started the fourth commandment with the word, "Remember." If we forget to commune with Him on His holy day, do we really love Him?

Now the devil cannot create life, so therefore, he can never be the Creator. However, he wants to be worshiped, so he came up with a devious plan to ensnare Christians. He substituted his day for the Lord's Day, and most Christians unknowingly bought into his counterfeit.

The Bible says that Satan is a deceiver, and the father of lies. "You are of your father the devil, and the desires of your father you want to do. He was a murderer from the beginning, and does not stand in the truth, because there is no truth in him. When he speaks a lie, he speaks from his own resources, for he is a liar and the father of it" John 8:44.

Jesus came with the truth, but John 1:11 says, "He came to His own, and His own did not receive Him." What a sad commentary the Bible gives of Jesus being rejected by His own church of the day! God's chosen people rejected Jesus, the chief cornerstone.

I submit to you that the Sabbath issue is not just about *a day;* it is about the acceptance or rejection of the chief cornerstone, Jesus Christ! The reason God wrote the Ten Commandments in stone is that, in the Bible, Jesus is referred to as the cornerstone! "Now, therefore, you are no longer strangers and foreigners, but fellow citizens with the saints and members of the household of God, having been built on the foundation of the apostles and prophets, Jesus Christ Himself being the chief cornerstone" Ephesians 2:19–20.

Jesus refers to Himself as the "rock" in Matthew 16:18, and David said in Psalm 118:22, "The stone which the builders rejected has become the chief cornerstone." The cornerstone is the strongest part of the entire building.

The Ten Commandment moral law of God will last for eternity. God's principles of life and love cannot be altered or changed. His Ten Commandments are a transcript of His own eternal character. Man cannot change God, His character, or His law.

Nailed to the Cross?
Now most Christians, both Protestant and Catholic, do not believe that it is necessary to set aside the seventh day of the week as a holy day of convocation to our Creator God. When confronted with the question as to why they don't

keep the seventh-day Sabbath, most Christians, including clergy, will tell you that it is no longer necessary to keep the fourth commandment, because they keep Sunday—the first day of the week—in honor of Christ's Resurrection. Some even call it the "New Testament Sabbath."

If you press the conversation further, most will tell you they don't live under the Old Testament Law, since it was nailed to the Cross. They're referring, of course, to Colossians 2:14, that reads, "Having wiped out the handwriting of requirements that was against us, which was contrary to us. And He has taken it out of the way, having nailed it to the cross." But try as one might, there's nothing in this verse that says the Ten Commandments were nailed to the Cross. Instead, it says, "Having wiped out the handwriting of requirements that was against us . . ."

We see a similar text in Ephesians 2:15, "Having abolished in His flesh the enmity, that is, the law of commandments contained in ordinances, so as to create in Himself one new man from the two, thus making peace."

Both of these texts talk about doing away with "the law of ordinances," not God's eternal Ten Commandment Law. The Jews had over 600 laws or ordinances that were to be followed. Praise God that Christ's death did away with these man-made laws!

So when someone tells me that they believe the Ten Commandments were nailed to the Cross, the next question I ask them is, "If the Ten Commandment Law was nailed to the Cross when Jesus was crucified, then does this mean it's okay for me to steal, kill, or commit adultery?"

I have yet to have anyone to tell me that they believe that it's okay to break any of the other nine commandments given on Mt. Sinai, even though they were given to Moses on the very same tables of stone as the others.

Living by Faith

Many people will tell you that New Testament Christians live by faith, and I agree that we all should live by faith, because the Bible does say that "the just shall live by faith" Hebrews 10:38. However, we do not make void the Ten Commandment Law to live by faith.

Let's hear what the Bible has to say about this controversial issue. The answer is found in Romans 3:31: "Do we then make void the law through faith? Certainly not! On the contrary, we establish the law." In other words, our faith in God *confirms* the Ten Commandment Law of God! There's the answer to the question. Don't you love the fact that the Bible does not leave us in the dark when we're looking for answers to pertinent questions about our salvation?

Satan's mission is to convince Christians that the Ten Commandment Law of God has been nailed to the Cross, thus releasing Christians from keeping or following them. And yes, sadly, he often uses "men of the cloth" as pawns for his deception.

But Jesus has not left us without weapons to combat the enemy. 2 Corinthians 10:4–5 says, "For the weapons of our warfare are not carnal but mighty in God for pulling down strongholds, casting down arguments and every high thing that exalts itself against the knowledge of God, bringing every thought into captivity to the obedience of Christ."

If you are one of those who believe the Ten Commandments were nailed to the Cross, or that all you need is to live by faith, then I encourage you to continue reading so we can clear this up. I'm sure that many honest-hearted Christians have never dealt with the Sabbath issue because they have never been confronted with the subject by anyone, or because they never thought it necessary.

Sidetracked by the Sabbath?

You may be asking why I seem to be getting sidetracked by talking about the fourth commandment, and I will tell you the answer: So far, we have shown that when a government (the State) negates or makes void God's commandments, they eventually end in national ruin. I also will submit to you that when the Church makes an attempt to change or negate God's Law, it, too, will fail.

I believe the Lord impressed me to write this book for such an hour as this. We have already seen the Supreme Court negate America's duty to uphold the sixth and seventh commandments—"You shall not murder" (abortion) and "You shall not commit adultery" (same-sex marriage). Both of these new laws of the State are in direct opposition to God's eternal Law of life—the Ten Commandments.

As a follower of Christ and His teachings, we have no authority to change or negate His eternal Ten Commandment Law. The Ten Commandments are a transcript of God's own character. So when we do away with, or try to change them, we are trying to make character adjustments to a holy and perfect God!

I'm glad that God has His people in all churches. As Christians, you and I are, by default, followers of truth. We are truth-seekers, and that is what defines us as Christians! In John 14:6, Jesus said, "I am the way, the truth, and the life. No one comes to the Father except through Me."

CHAPTER IX

THE GREAT CONTROVERSY

There is a great controversy going on between Christ and Satan as to the ownership of our souls! One Scripture passage we just read tells us that Satan is the father of lies, and another tells us that Jesus is the way, the truth, and the life. This is stated very clearly in John 10:10: "The thief does not come except to steal, and to kill, and to destroy. I have come that they may have life, and that they may have it more abundantly."

Just like the other nine, the Sabbath Commandment is not going away, and it must be dealt with. You will face the question of its sanctity now or later, for it will come to the surface in these closing moments of Earth's history. By studying and finding the truth now, you can be prepared to deal with the Sabbath issue when Sunday worship becomes the law of the land in the near future.

Now I'd like to delve into why I've said this is a much bigger issue than a Saturday versus Sunday day of worship.

The Sabbath Commandment is found in the middle of the Ten Commandments. Remember that it is, in fact, the cornerstone.

Now let's deal with it from this perspective: If the fourth commandment can be dismissed or done away with by modern-day Christians, then why can't any of the other nine commandments be dismissed or done away with? Or can they? Wouldn't you agree that's a fair question?

In Exodus 20, the Lord gave Moses the Ten Commandments. The Ten Commandments are a transcript of God's character—they represent Who He is! He is a God of love, and a God of order. However, there has been much discussion in the Christian world about to whom the Ten Commandments apply. God gave them to Moses to give to the Israelites following their release from over 400 years of captivity in Egypt. Therefore, many Christians contend that this "Law of Moses" was intended for the Hebrews, or the nation of Israel.

Since many Christian leaders maintain that the Ten Commandment Law of God was nailed to the Cross, they contend that, "We are not under law, but under grace." Yet, most Christians believe that it is important to keep the other nine commandments, so there is really only one commandment they believe was "nailed to the cross"—the fourth commandment, pertaining to God's instructions to His people to keep the seventh-day Sabbath (Saturday) holy.

It seems we should decide who takes ownership of the seventh-day Sabbath before we remove it from the rest of the commandments, don't you think? Was the Sabbath only given to the Israelites? Is it truly just the "Jewish Sabbath," as many Christians commonly refer it? Or is it the Sabbath of Jehovah God?

If the Sabbath belongs to the Jews, then I must confess that New Testament Christians should be released from adhering to or the keeping the Sabbath holy, but let's see what the Bible says about to whom the Sabbath belongs. Exodus 20:10 says, "But the seventh day is the Sabbath of the Lord your God." From this we can see that when God introduced the children of Israel to the Sabbath, He also claimed ownership. He didn't say, "I'm giving you your own Jewish Sabbath for Jews to keep," right?

Let's look back to Genesis 2:1–3, where the Bible says, "Thus the heavens and the earth, and all the host of them, were finished. And on the seventh day God ended His work which He had done, and He rested on the seventh day from all His work which He had done. Then God blessed the seventh day and sanctified it, because in it He rested from all His work which God had created and made."

According to these texts in Genesis and Exodus, the seventh-day Sabbath could not be a Jewish Sabbath, since it was already in existence well over 2,000 years before there was ever a Jew. On the seventh day of Creation, God ended His work and rested on the Sabbath. That's pretty straightforward and simple to understand, isn't it?

Now let's read Isaiah 58:13–14. Here God says, "If you turn away your foot from the Sabbath, from doing your pleasure on My holy day, and call the Sabbath a delight, the holy day of the Lord honorable, and shall honor Him, not doing your own ways, nor finding your own pleasure, nor speaking your own words, then you shall delight yourself in the Lord; and I will cause you to ride on the high hills of the earth, and feed you with the heritage of Jacob your father. The mouth of the Lord has spoken."

Each of these texts refers to the seventh-day Sabbath as *God's* holy day, not man's. In Isaiah 58:13, He even says, "On My holy day." There's no mention of this being a Jewish or man-made Sabbath. In fact, Jesus Himself said to the Pharisees, "The Sabbath was made for man, and not man for the Sabbath. Therefore the Son of Man is also Lord of the Sabbath" Mark 2:27–28.

Once again, we see that God is the author of the Sabbath, and that *it was made for man*—and not just for the Jews!

The Lord's Day

Many Christians will tell you, that in the New Testament, the Lord's Day is on Sunday, not Saturday, the seventh day of the week, so let's examine what the Scriptures say. The text they are referring to is found in Revelation 1:10, and it says, "I was in the Spirit on the Lord's Day."

We have already established that Jesus is the Lord of the Sabbath, and that the Lord's Day is the seventh-day Sabbath, not Sunday, the first day of the week. In fact, *there's not a single Scripture reference to Sunday as the Lord's Day in all the Bible!*

There is a spiritual war going on today here in America and around the world. Satan's plan is to substitute God's fourth commandment with one of his own that will cause multitudes of Christians to worship him, instead of their Creator God! If successful, he will finally receive the worship, glory, and praise he has coveted since before he was cast out of Heaven.

Can't We Pick and Choose?

God did not give the Ten Commandments for us to pick and choose what we want. As Christians, we either keep them all, or according to the Bible, we break them all! The book of James is very clear about this: "For whoever shall keep the whole law, and yet stumble in one point, he is guilty of all" James 2:10.

Let's look at it like this: If a bicycle has a chain made up of ten links, and any one of the links breaks, the whole chain is broken! It is the same with the Ten Commandments. If we break any of them, we are guilty of rebelling against all of them, and we only have to be in rebellion against one commandment to be guilty of rebelling against God.

What Satan Hates

Satan hates the two institutions established at Creation: the Sabbath and marriage. Why? Because when we keep the seventh-day Sabbath, we are worshiping the true God of the Sabbath, who gave us this special day to set aside our busy schedule and spend time in communion with Him. Satan hates the seventh-day Sabbath because God's fourth commandment contains His seal of authority.

At the same time, Satan hates marriage between one man and one woman and is waging a spiritual war against it. His plan is to destroy the line between male and female genders, and, if he succeeds, he can make void the whole Genesis account of Creation! If God did not create Adam and Eve male and female, then God does not exist, re-enforcing the longtime lie of evolution! If Satan can use man-made institutions and governments to promote the entire gay, lesbian, and transgender agenda, then he becomes the god they worship!

When any nation, government—or church, for that matter—replaces God's agenda with Satan's agenda, this is a slap in the face to our Creator God, and they will pay the consequence of their choices.

Satan has already deceived multitudes of Christians into following him by substituting a day of worship that originates with the father of lies, and not the Creator of the Universe; and now he is bent on setting up his own kingdom on earth, and his subjects will worship him, in spite of themselves.

Thankfully, our loving and merciful God has held back the winds of strife and given us ample time to turn to the Book of all books—the Holy Bible—and search it for truth. But as in the days of Noah, God will not strive with men forever (Genesis 6:3). When Jesus returns to this earth the second time, He will come back as King of kings and Lord of lords. He will take to Heaven all those who have surrendered their lives to Him and followed His eternal Law of love, and there they will rule and reign with Him forever.

The Sabbath is not just about a day. It's about obedience to God. When Jesus comes back to claim His children, whose side will you be on? Our destiny won't be decided when Jesus returns. Our destiny is being decided right now! The question we should be asking ourselves is, "Do I love Jesus enough to follow Him all the way?"

"Winking" at Ignorance

I'm glad we serve a loving God! 1 John 4:7–8 says, "Beloved, let us love one another, for love is of God; and everyone who loves is born of God and knows God. He who does not love does not know God, for God is love."

He is a gracious God, as well! Acts 17:30 says, "And the times of this ignorance God winked at; but now commandeth all men everywhere to repent." I'm also glad that God "winks" at our ignorance by not holding us accountable for breaking His law *until we know* that we are breaking His law, aren't you?

Let me explain it like this for those who may still be struggling with what I am saying: Each of us, as we grow older, is defined by our character. At a funeral, for instance, a family member will often give a life sketch of the individual who passed away, based on that person's character during his lifetime. This is never based on one good or bad thing that he or she may have done in life. I have yet to hear a life sketch at someone's funeral where their loved ones dwelt on the bad things the deceased may have done in their past, have you? This person may have done some bad things, but the good outweighs the bad, which is why the life sketch is based on that person's character over a lifetime.

And so it is with God. He considers everything about us and takes into account our inherited and acquired tendencies. He knows our hearts, and judges us fairly and righteously. We can always trust in His justice and mercy.

CHAPTER
X

STANDING FOR WHAT'S RIGHT

After studying this subject for many years, I find it interesting that many Christians disapproved when the United States government rejected God's sixth and seventh commandments and made abortion and same-sex marriage the law of the land. In fact, I believe that if I were to walk into any number of Christian worship services and ask for a show of hands from those who believe that it is *pleasing* to God to kill babies, or for men to marry men and women to marry women, very few hands would be raised in support. Don't you agree? However, millions of these same Christians voted for political leaders who championed abortion and same-sex marriage into law!

Since you already know that I am an independent when it comes to politics, please don't accuse me of choosing sides between the Democrats and Republicans. Instead, my point is this: *As Christians, we must stand on the side of what's right, based on Bible principles. We cannot allow our tradition or political leanings to distort our Christianity.*

In the 2016 election, Christians who voted for leaders supporting same-sex marriage and abortion told me specifically *why* they voted that way. Most of them justified their voting against God's Ten Commandment Law because they did not like the other candidate or thought the other party didn't care about the needs of the poor and minorities.

This may or may not be true, and I am not here to defend any earthly organization that does not hold up the Bible as the rule of life, but my parents used to say, "Two wrongs don't make a right!" Are any of you old enough to have heard that from your parents? Because this old saying is based on a principle of right doing from the Bible, it still holds true today!

Justifying Our Choices

Now, I'm sure some Christians are a little unhappy with me, because they want to justify why they would cast a vote for a candidate or political party that endorses and promotes same-sex marriage and abortion. If you are one of them, let's reason this out together. Some of you who voted this way are Christians who believe that God gave us Ten Commandments to live by—including the fourth commandment, which commands us to keep God's seventh-day Sabbath holy.

Let me start by asking you a hypothetical question: If there is a candidate from either party in the next election who supports and promotes that America should have a National Sunday Law designating Sunday as a day of rest in America, would you vote for them? I'm going to guess that most of you would answer no.

If this is so, then I'll ask another question: What if you believed the candidate or party on the opposing side does not care about the needs of the poor and the minorities? Would you still vote for the party who is openly campaigning to enforce Sunday as a day of rest as the law of the land? If not, then, why not? Isn't this the same logic used to vote for candidates and parties in the 2012 and 2016 elections who campaigned by openly endorsing same-sex marriage and promising to make it the law of the land—which did happen?

The question we must ask ourselves before we attempt to present truth to others is this: Is keeping the fourth commandment—or any commandment—more important than keeping any of the others? I think we can agree that all Ten Commandments were given by God and that we are not saved by keeping the Ten Commandments. Instead, we are saved by the blood of the Lamb and our willingness to accept His blood as an atonement for our sins.

I've learned something in my 65-plus years of life—truth is always truth! Truth will not compromise to fit my earthly reasoning, wants, or fleshly desires! So the point of this conversation is this: Christians who keep the fourth commandment, "Remember the Sabbath day to keep it holy," should also realize that all of the commandments apply to them including the sixth and seventh concerning abortion and same-sex marriage. Another old saying that applies here is, "We can't have it both ways!" We cannot pick and choose which of the commandments we want to follow, any more than people who decide they don't have to obey God's fourth commandment.

If I still have any readers, let's move on.

CHAPTER
XI

I WANT TO KNOW TRUTH

I told you at the beginning of this book that I'm sick and tired of political correctness, so I'm not going to deal with this subject in a politically correct manner. I will deal with it, however, based on the Bible, and I'll welcome your opinion otherwise. You see, *I want to know truth.* My word is not truth unless it stands on God's Word—and neither is yours. We are all sinners in need of a Savior, and we must all come to the foot of the Cross to find forgiveness. So I'm not pointing a finger at you without three fingers pointing back at me.

However, once we have done this, and have found forgiveness from our sins, Jesus commissions us to "Go ye" into all the world, teaching all nations about His saving power (Matthew 28:18–20).

Our goal is to become one with Christ, but the devil has other plans to distract us from fulfilling our mission of taking the gospel to the world. During Pentecost, the Bible says in Acts 2:1 that the disciples came together "with one accord," and in Acts 4:32 it says, "All the believers were one in heart and mind." In other words, they were like-minded about taking the gospel to the world.

I ask people to really pray to God for wisdom before joining one political party or another. I have seen churches divided over politics, and I've seen Christian Facebook friends publicly argue with each other over politics. Do we, as Christians, really want to be members of a political party—or a religious organization, for that matter—that believes God's Law is inadequate, and undermines the Lawgiver Himself by attempting to change or negate His holy Law? Hopefully this answer is a resounding *No!*

Don't you want to be part of the Christian body that will stand up for what's right and be willing to give your life unto death, if necessary, for the cause of God? We should be willing to live by and protect God's Law with our life's blood, just as Jesus gave His life's blood to protect and ensure our future of eternity in Heaven.

As Christians, we do not have to fear the future. All we have to do is read the back of the Book to find out that, in the end, we win! So let's read it: "And they overcame him [Satan] by the blood of the Lamb and by the word of their testimony, and they did not love their lives to the death" Revelation 12:11.

Coming Out of "Babylon"

Jesus is coming back for a purified bride—a people who "did not love their lives to the death" for the cause of God. The world cannot know truth if God's people are part of Babylon—or spiritual confusion!

Revelation 18:4 says, "And I heard another voice from heaven saying, 'Come out of her, my people, lest you share in her sins, and lest you receive of her plagues.'" Instead of being part of spiritual confusion, Jesus wants us to come out of Babylon and rightly represent His character. He wants the world to see that He is *the only way off* of this planet, where sin, disease, death, and destruction reign supreme!

In Revelation 14, the Bible describes the end-times message for an end-times people to proclaim. It comes in the form of three angels flying in the midst of heaven—each with a warning message sent by a God of love to planet Earth's inhabitants!

God is sending His people a love letter that says, "Here I come, ready or not." Just as it appears as though the devil is about to make God's Law void, Jesus intervenes, saying, "Don't be discouraged. Stay close to Me, and I will stay close to you. Look up! Your redemption draws nigh!"

We are living in the closing moments of Earth's history. And how can I say that with confidence? Because the Bible gives us the signs that the end of this world is near. But we will only see these signs if we're digging into God's Word every day. Prophecy was given for a reason. God is telling us in advance what the devil is doing to deceive the inhabitants of this earth. He is also giving us directions on how to escape the death trap Satan has set to kill, steal, and destroy us!

Finding Peace

When we look around, we see wars and strife like never before. Ungodliness, as in the days of Noah before the flood, and unnatural affections run rampant, as they did in Sodom and Gomorrah! If Jesus doesn't come back in the near future, man will succeed in destroying the earth and everything in it. The United States of America has enough nuclear weapons to destroy life as we know it on our planet, if all of them were discharged at once. Russia and China have a tremendous arsenal of weaponry that could do almost as much damage, and smaller countries such as Iran and North Korea are also developing nuclear weapons.

Make no mistake, we are living in perilous times, and unless we are studying God's Word, we will not even realize the danger upon us. Looking through physical eyes, we cannot find peace in this troubled world. However, when we look through spiritual glasses, we will always find peace in the midst of the storm.

A couple of years ago, the Lord gave me a song. I'd written a number of them before, but when I wrote this one, tears began streaming down my face. I was deeply moved, because as I was writing, I felt God directing my hands to pen the words He chose for this song.

The song is entitled, "Just In Time," and here are the lyrics:

There were famines and earthquakes
With trouble all around
The heavens did shake
No peace could be found

There were wars and strife
On every hand
It seemed God had lost
With no hope for man

"Where is your God?" the demons cried
"He's left you here to die
Your truth has failed
It's all been a lie"

But a shout from Heaven
Can now be heard.
It came from God,
the Living Word!

And just in time, the Savior came
Just in time He called my name!
Salvation's plan for fallen man
Redemption by the Great I AM.

When you're discouraged, remember the words of Isaiah 54:17: "'No weapon formed against you shall prosper, and every tongue which rises against you in judgment you shall condemn. This is the heritage of the servants of the Lord, and their righteousness is from Me,' says the Lord."

No harm can rob us of our eternity with Jesus Christ. When we put on the armor of God, nothing can penetrate it!

CHAPTER
XII

MESSAGES FROM GOD

In His love for fallen man, God has always spoken to us through holy men, as they were inspired by the Holy Spirit. However, most Christian churches have failed to read these love letters sent by God in the book of Revelation, through the pen of John the Revelator.

Revelation 14 depicts three angels flying in the midst of heaven. Each angel has a message for the last generation of people on planet Earth. The first angel's message is about worship; the second angel's message is about Babylon and spiritual confusion; and the third angel's message is about the Mark of the Beast. These messages, when properly interpreted, should bring us peace and joy. Why? Because they tell us that if we are faithful to God and His Word, no power on earth can defeat us!

The three angels of Revelation 14, along with a fourth angel in Revelation 18, give us a road map and a glimpse into the future. Their messages give a loud and clear call to all who are seeking truth in the closing moments of Earth's history, and they counteract the counterfeit religions that have fallen into the confusion of Babylon. But their messages also assure us that if we love God more than ourselves, He will bring us through the final battle of this Great Controversy between Good and Evil. Satan and sin will be forever gone, and the saints of God will be forever saved!

The First Angel's Message
Over the years, I've sometimes found that being a layman has its advantages when talking to lay people, since I'm not likely to spiritually talk over their heads. So let me try to comment on these angels' messages, and why I believe they are relevant for modern-day Christians. (Remember, this is not intended to be an in-depth study of Revelation 14, but merely an overview of its relevance for us today.)

Let's start with a short overview of the first angel's message, found in Revelation 14:6–7: "Then I saw another angel flying in the midst of heaven, having the everlasting gospel to preach to those who dwell on the earth—to every nation, tribe, tongue, and people—saying with a loud voice, 'Fear God and give glory to Him, for the hour of His judgment has come; and worship Him who made heaven and earth, the sea and springs of water.'"

The first angel's warning message is telling us how best to prepare for the coming destruction of planet Earth and its inhabitants, which is even now being orchestrated by Satan. But first, the good news: True followers of Christ have nothing to fear! Isaiah 43:1–3 says, "Fear not, for I have redeemed you; I have called you by your name; you are Mine. When you pass through the waters, I will be with you; and through the rivers, they shall not overflow you. When you walk through the fire, you shall not be burned, nor shall the flame scorch you. For I am the Lord your God, the Holy One of Israel, your Savior."

The first angel proclaims a coming judgment to the world:

The Earth's inhabitants will be judged according to whom they worship. In other words, as human beings, we are the focal point of the Great Controversy between Christ and Satan (or between Good and Evil). The first angel directs God's people to worship the Creator God of the Universe—the only true God.

In order to be prepared, we first need to be warned about the coming disaster, right? This is what these three angels are doing. They are blowing the trumpet, giving God's remnant people a warning to prepare for a spiritual battle. So how do we prepare?

Let's read Ephesians 6:11–12: "Put on the whole armor of God, that you may be able to stand against the wiles of the devil. For we do not wrestle against flesh and blood, but against principalities, against powers, against the rulers of the darkness of this age, against spiritual hosts of wickedness in the heavenly places." It is imperative that we worship the true Creator God of Heaven.

People worship millions of false gods. But none of these gods created the heavens and the Earth, and they did not create human life. I've been to India, where they claim to worship several million gods. For most Christians, it is easy to see the futility of this kind of worship, where men create their own gods by inventing all kinds of man-made objects, and then worship their own creations! By contrast, in Christianity, we worship the Creator of Heaven and Earth as the true and everlasting God. As Christians, we use the Bible, and the Bible only, as our spiritual guide. We will not be deceived into worshiping man-made objects or false gods! Why?

The devil will not tempt us in our strong areas. He will always come at us in our weakest areas. For instance, I've never smoked cigarettes, nor have I ever tasted any alcohol, so I'm never tempted with either one. However, if I have a pride problem, *he will tempt me there*; and if I have a temper, *he will tempt me to lose control.* The devil doesn't care that I don't smoke or drink, and he will only tempt me in the spiritually weaker areas of my life. He doesn't care what area of life I fail in, as long as I fail. His whole purpose is to "help us" fall from grace, and as Christians, we can be sure that he is out "to steal, to kill, and to destroy" John 10:10.

Is it possible for Christians to go to church, sing, pray, and worship God, only to find that it was all false worship? Let's go to the Bible for the answer and read what Jesus said in Mark 7:5–9: "Then the Pharisees and scribes asked Him, 'Why do Your disciples not walk according to the tradition of the elders, but eat bread with unwashed hands?' He answered and said to them, 'Well did Isaiah prophesy of you hypocrites, as it is written: "This people honors Me with their lips, but their heart is far from Me. And in vain they worship Me, teaching as doctrines the commandments of men." For laying aside the commandment of God, you hold the tradition of men—the washing of pitchers and cups, and many other such things you do.' He said to them, 'All too well you reject the commandment of God, that you may keep your tradition.'"

Wow! Jesus is talking to the *religious leaders* of His day, not people who did not claim to know the Creator God. These were folks who probably tithed faithfully, were well-versed in the Scriptures, and attended the synagogue regularly. Yet, Jesus confronted them about the futility of their actions and the emptiness of their hearts.

Road Signs
A number of years ago, my daughter and her family visited me from Nashville, Tennessee. I'd said goodbye to them as they pulled out of my driveway and headed home, but about three hours later, she called me to say they were almost all the way to Memphis! They sincerely thought they would be in Nashville by then, but by not paying attention to the road

signs, they ended up on the wrong road, which did not take them home.

Another old saying says something like this: "The road to hell will be paved with sincere people who had good intentions." However, we need not be discouraged, since Jesus says through His prophet, "And you will seek Me and find Me, when you search for Me with all your heart" Jeremiah 29:13. The Bible is full of road signs, and if we follow Jesus, we won't be deceived.

Our road to eternal salvation is a process of sanctification, and the Greek word that is translated "sanctification" (*hagiasmos*) means "holiness." Therefore, to sanctify means "to make holy." It's important to understand that we cannot make ourselves holy. Only God can do that, because, by nature, we are born sinful: "For all have sinned and fall short of the glory of God" Romans 3:23. However, the good news in the Bible is that "If we confess our sins, He is faithful and just to forgive us our sins and to cleanse us from all unrighteousness" 1 John 1:9.

In order for God to mold us into His image during this lifelong process of sanctification, we need to be willing "vessels for honor" (2 Timothy 2:21). Salvation is between you and God. Please don't look to men, but keep your eyes on Jesus and His Word, the Bible.

In Matthew 7:21–23, Jesus says, "Not everyone who says to Me, 'Lord, Lord,' shall enter the kingdom of heaven, but he who does the will of My Father in heaven. Many will say to Me in that day, 'Lord, Lord, have we not prophesied in Your name, cast out demons in Your name, and done many wonders in Your name?' And then I will declare to them, 'I never knew you; depart from Me, you who practice lawlessness!'"

This seems to include men of the cloth—people who prophesy, cast out demons, and do wonderful works. Yet Jesus says, "I never knew you; depart from Me, you who practice lawlessness!"

In the eighth chapter of the book of John, the Pharisees, or Jewish religious leaders, sought to trick Jesus into either speaking against God's Law, or the laws of the land, by asking Him cunning questions regarding what should be done to a woman who was caught in adultery. However, Jesus revealed their true motives by kneeling in the dust and writing their sins in the sand. Later, He referred to Himself as the "light of the world," and said that He followed the will of His Father. His words were so filled with truth that the Bible says many believed in Him (John 8:30). Encouraging them further, Jesus said to those who believed, "If you abide in My word, you are My disciples indeed. And you shall know the truth, and the truth shall make you free" John 8:31–32.

But while His words brought hope to those who believed in Him, they incensed the religious leaders, who replied with angry insults. Finally, after all hope of reaching them was gone, Jesus said, "You are of your father the devil, and the desires of your father you want to do. He was a murderer from the beginning, and does not stand in the truth, because there is no truth in him. When he speaks a lie, he speaks from his own resources, for he is a liar and the father of it" John 8:44.

It would be well for us to consider whom Jesus was speaking to when He said, "You are of your father the devil." Was He speaking to Satan's angels? Was He speaking to non-believers? No, *He was speaking to the very ones who professed to believe and follow God*—the religious leaders of the day. The apostle John wrote, "He came to His own, and His own did not receive Him" John 1:11. What a sad commentary the Bible gives of Jesus being rejected by His own church! God's chosen people rejected Jesus—"the chief cornerstone" Psalm 118:22.

I don't want to be one of those who reject Jesus Christ, and I'm sure you don't either, or you wouldn't be reading this little book. So how can we be sure that we are not like those mentioned in the Scriptures who rejected Jesus, the cornerstone and foundation of the world?

Once again, Jesus answers this question with, "If you love Me, keep My commandments" John 14:15. And then later, the Bible says, "For this is the love of God, that we keep His commandments. And His commandments are not burdensome" 1 John 5:3.

Satan is amazingly deceptive in his working through men and women. Matthew 24:24 says, "For false christs and false prophets will rise and show great signs and wonders to deceive, if possible, even the elect." As we found out through the first angel's message, God instructs us not to worship false gods, but to worship Him, the Creator God of the Universe.

The Second Angel's Message

The second angel brings another proclamation for planet Earth's inhabitants. Revelation 14:8 says, "And another angel followed, saying, 'Babylon is fallen, is fallen, that great city, because she has made all nations drink of the wine of the wrath of her fornication.' "

A few chapters later, the Bible mentions a fourth angel's message: "And I heard another voice from heaven saying, 'Come out of her, my people, lest you share in her sins, and lest you receive of her plagues. For her sins have reached to heaven, and God has remembered her iniquities'" Revelation 18:4–5.

The book of Revelation reveals a great conflict between truth and error. There are two systems of worship: God wants us to worship Him "in spirit and in truth" (John 4:23–24), while Babylon—representing religious confusion, wants us to worship false gods.

In Revelation's prophecies, a pure, chaste woman represents the true church (see Revelation 12:1–2), and a harlot represents the fallen church. God's true church—the Bride of Christ—is victorious and reflects the glory of God by revealing His truth to the world. The apostate church, on the other hand, offers up her wine of false doctrines, confusing the minds of multitudes and leading them to destruction.

The second angel of Revelation 14 and the fourth angel of Revelation 18 both cry out to the inhabitants of the earth to worship the only true Creator God. We are not only to come out of churches that teach false doctrines, but we ourselves are to be temples of the Holy Spirit where Jesus may rule and reign supreme in our lives. Only through true worship will we find victory in Christ!

It is worth noting here that the second angel does not say that "all nations drink of the wine of the wrath of her fornication—except the United States of America." Instead, the second angel declares that *all* the nations drink from that wine! This wine is the wine of spiritual deception.

Of course, I understand that the United States of America wasn't a nation at that time, but I also know that the book of Revelation is the *revelation of Jesus Christ*—the Alpha and Omega, the first and the last, the beginning and the end. It is also a book that contains prophecy about future events.

Earlier in this book, we looked up the dictionary definition of *deceit*, but *spiritual deceit* is what the three angels of Revelation 14 are warning about. It is led by earthly governments and religious leaders, including whole churches. And remember, if it were *blatant* rebellion against God's law, it wouldn't be deception.

The Third Angel's Message

Let's continue with a brief description of the third angel's message to a lost and dying world. "Then a third angel followed them, saying with a loud voice, 'If anyone worships the beast and his image, and receives his mark on his forehead or on his hand, he himself shall also drink of the wine of the wrath of God, which is poured out full strength into the cup of His indignation. He shall be tormented with fire and brimstone in the presence of the holy angels and in the presence of the Lamb'" Revelation 14:9–10.

In order to understand the significance of this beast, his

image, and those who receive his mark on their foreheads, we would need to do an in-depth study of the books of Daniel and Revelation. This would be beyond the scope of this book, and rather than try to immerse you into a deep Bible prophecy study, I'd like to point you to the **3ABN.tv** website for further investigation. However, I will give you the short version of this beast of Revelation 14 by saying that it represents a religious power that rises up from the earth and *deceives* its inhabitants into "following" or worshiping a religious organization instead of the true Creator God. This religious organization has sought to change God's times and law (see Daniel 7:25)!

The beast stands in the place of God, and the image to the beast represent the churches that worship this beast, and bow down to it. This action of false worship causes the people in those churches to receive a mark on their foreheads or in their hands.

Our Creator God does not accept false worship, and if we're guilty of false worship, we cannot enter Heaven. We read some texts earlier that made this clear to us, but imagine the sadness Jesus felt as He quoted the words of the prophet in Isaiah 29:13, "These people draw near to Me with their mouth, and honor Me with their lips, but their heart is far from Me. And in vain they worship Me, teaching as doctrines the commandments of men" Matthew 15:8–9.

The important thing for us to understand right now is that God loves us and has made a plan of redemption for fallen man. All we have to do is *accept His free gift of salvation.* To do this, we must first accept the fact that we are sinners (Romans 3:23) and confess our sins (1 John 1:9). Next, we must go and tell the world about the good news of redemption through the blood of the Lord Jesus Christ (Matthew 28:8–10).

The third angel's message of Revelation 14 may be the most solemn warning given to God's last day remnant people on planet Earth, and in order to prepare for a spiritual battle, we must be able to discern truth from error. We can only do that as we submit and commit our lives to Jesus Christ, so He may work in us and through us.

Now, I'll tell you again that *I believe that God has people in all churches!* It is very important for us to realize that we cannot judge anyone by outward appearances, since the Bible says that man looks on the outward appearance, but God looks on the heart (1 Samuel 16:7).

God gave John the Revelator a vision down through the ages—all the way to the Second Coming of Christ. It was given in symbols that were used throughout the Old Testament, which every Jewish child learned from their earliest years. However, in today's world, many Christian churches discount the books of Daniel and Revelation as irrelevant for twenty-first-century Christians. *Nothing could be further from the truth!* Instead, the books of Daniel and Revelation hold the keys to understanding the Great Controversy between Christ and Satan that has been going on for thousands of years.

The three angels' messages of Revelation 14 are our road map to eternal life, and that's why it is so important to understand all we can about these prophecies. They give great solace to the Christian, because when we read and understand them, we begin to see how much Jesus really loves us, and that He's made a way of escape for those who follow Him. But in order to understand this fully, we must be willing to study God's Word to find truth.

At first, this may seem a little overwhelming to a new Christian, or to those whose churches do not see the relevance of these prophecies. However, as you study Revelation, I believe you will find that:

1. Revelation is a book that reveals the true character of Christ and that God is love.

2. Revelation exposes Satan's plan for the destruction of mankind—but also reveals God's plan to save us for eternity.

3. We hold the key to our own salvation. It is our choice, and we must make a conscious decision of whom we will serve. We are either on one side or the other. To whom will we pledge our allegiance?

4. Most importantly, the prophecies of Daniel and Revelation show that when we submit and commit our lives to Christ and follow the teachings of the Bible, we will never be deceived by spiritual vigilantes who have sought to change God's eternal Ten Commandment Law!

I like to say the gospel is all about "Come and Go." First we come to the foot of the Cross and confess our sins, and then we go and tell what Christ has done for us. *Your personal testimony is your greatest asset in your witness for Christ.* The world didn't give it to you, and the world can't take it away!

In closing, I pray God's richest blessings on your life as you worship Him in spirit and in truth.

PROLOGUE

I believe that you are a seeker of truth or you would not have read this book. The Bible says, "And you shall know the truth, and the truth shall make you free" John 8:32.

In closing, I would like for you to keep in mind that for the Christian truth-seeker, it is easier to be "saved" than "lost." The only way Christians can be lost is if they take their eyes off of the Word of God, which is the road map to Heaven.

The Bible says, "For false christs and false prophets will rise and show great signs and wonders to deceive, if possible, even the elect" Matthew 24:24. This simply means that just because you may be a pastor, a church elder, a missionary, or someone who has spent their entire life serving the Lord, the devil is still out to deceive you!

The good news is, if we stay focused on our relationship with the Lord Jesus Christ and are continually seeking truth, the devil cannot harm us. He may rob us of many earthly things, but he cannot rob us of our eternity with the Lord Jesus Christ! We belong to our Creator God, and as long as we stay faithful to Him, Heaven and eternal life are assured!

Let's read John 14:1–3: "Let not your heart be troubled; you believe in God, believe also in Me. In My Father's house are many mansions; if it were not so, I would have told you. I go to prepare a place for you. And if I go and prepare a place for you, I will come again and receive you to Myself; that where I am, there you may be also." Isn't this wonderful news?

And lastly, let's read Revelation 22:13–14: "'I am the Alpha and the Omega, the Beginning and the End, the First and the Last.' Blessed are those who do His commandments, that they may have the right to the tree of life, and may enter through the gates into the city."

I plan to be there. What about you?